TALKING BACK
PUPIL VIEWS ON DISAFFECTION

by

KAY KINDER
ALISON WAKEFIELD
ANNE WILKIN

Published in May 1996
by the National Foundation for Educational Research,
The Mere, Upton Park, Slough, Berkshire SL1 2DQ

CONTENTS

INTRODUCTION

BACKGROUND

GEST funding for 1995-96 in the category 'Truancy and Disaffected Pupils' has been granted to some 90 LEAs, and, of these, over 70 have used the word 'disaffection' in the title of their bid. This no doubt reflects a view that the problem of pupil disengagement from school is a serious one and that initiatives need to address a range of disaffected behaviours, as well as non-attendance.

Indeed, the focus of these GEST-funded initiatives shows much variety, as already demonstrated by the 1993-94 and 1994-95 GEST programme evaluation for the DFEE by Learmonth (1995), and by the audit of school-based strategies which the NFER project 'School Attendance, Truancy and Exclusions' reported in its first discussion paper, *Three To Remember* (Kinder *et al.*, 1995). Such an array of initiatives would in turn suggest there is recognition of a wide range of factors underpinning disaffection.

This short report is the second from the NFER project referenced above and looks at pupil perspectives on the issue of disaffection.

A growing number of studies are attempting to explore the views and experiences of pupils, for instance Ruddock *et al.* (1996) and Davie and Galloway (1996). To date, some of the most notable research on pupils' perceptions of disaffection have either used survey approaches (e.g. ILEA, 1984; Stoll and O'Keefe, 1989), selected samples from just one year group (Gray and Jesson, 1990), or chosen to look at disaffected males only (Chaplain, 1996).

This discussion paper attempts to reflect the views of a wide range of pupils garnered through interview, and, in their own vernacular, convey the issues they raised. It also tries to address how such perspectives might be significant for the educational professionals, at school and LEA level, who continue to work with and support disaffected youngsters.

THE SAMPLE AND ITS SELECTION

In the second phase of the NFER project, the views of 160 young people from 20 schools and two special off-site units were gathered. Very nearly all of these had a history of truancy and/or disruption and therefore were recipients of at least one aspect of their school's initiatives on disaffection.

Each institution was asked to provide up to eight pupil interviewees who had involvement in the initiative(s) to deal with attendance and/or behaviour issues. Because of this, and perhaps reflecting the gender bias of disaffected behaviour, the final sample showed a preponderance of boys, especially in the lower secondary school. The type and severity of disaffection which the sample exhibited was broad-ranging. There were examples of long-term school-refusers, pupils excluded permanently for disruptive behaviour, as well as those whose emerging behaviour and/or attendance patterns were identified by the school as a potential cause for concern. As such, the sample can claim at least to reflect a genuine voice of the disaffected school pupil. In terms of age and gender, the sample could be broken down as follows:

	Male	Female	Total
Primary	14	9	23
Lower secondary (Y7-9)	48	28	76
Upper secondary (Y10 upwards)	30	31	61
Total	92	68	160

THE INTERVIEW

Each pupil was interviewed individually for about 35 minutes. The questions covered:

* views on the causes of truancy and disruptive behaviour in school;
* personal experiences and involvement in both these aspects of disaffection;

* attitudes to and experience of exclusion (fixed-term and permanent);
* views on the impact of any school-based strategies to address disaffection which they had encountered, including their institution's general reward and sanctions system; and
* improvements they could envisage.

All the interviews were conducted in privacy during school time, and with strong assurances of the right to confidentiality and anonymity. The research team was well aware of the sensitivity of asking pupils directly to divulge information about activities which could be seen as essentially anti-authority or even non-legal. Equally, probing what lay behind their disaffected behaviour could on occasion uncover extraordinarily difficult home circumstances and/or severe emotional problems. In some of these instances, pupils were clearly unwilling or unable to talk in depth on such personal matters. However, most did so, and the structure of the interview was intended to ensure that all pupils could also speak generally about the issues surrounding school disaffection, as well as comment on the nature and effectiveness of the measures in place within school to counter it.

This second report deals exclusively with the pupils' perceptions of causes and their personal experiences of disaffected behaviours. Further reports will include the data on pupils' perceptions of exclusions, and their evaluative comment on the specific disaffection initiative(s) with which they were involved.

ISSUES IN INTERVIEWING PUPILS ABOUT DISAFFECTION

Finally, before presenting the findings in full, some general points or caveats about the interview methodology need to be acknowledged.

First, it might be suggested that pupils cannot always fully recognise the reasons that underpin their actions. There is then the issue as to whether they can accurately relay motivations for anti-school behaviour, especially to an unknown person in a one-off interview situation, however much the interviewer may try to convey neutrality and 'unconditional positive regard'. It is at least possible that nominating 'friends' as an influence upon disaffected behaviour reflects this misrecognition or guardedness: as all teachers and parents know, assertions that the locus of control (and hence 'blame') is beyond themselves is a fairly typical child response. The fact there was a low incidence of pupils citing factors within the individual/personality domain could also perhaps corroborate this. (However, the significance of pupils' replying with accounts of their own role and responsibility for disaffected behaviour will be returned to.) Equally, some of the responses may represent that exaggerated and 'cool' bravado which can also be typical of disaffected pupils' self-presentation.

Whatever the methodological and substantive drawbacks, granting validity and listening seriously to the viewpoints and accounts of young people who had displayed some degree of disaffected behaviour was nevertheless seen as important. They represented the possibility of new insights into the causes of - and hence solutions to - the serious problem of truancy and disruption. While many of the responses will not be in any way 'new' to teachers and other education professionals, it is hoped that the weight of evidence from a substantial sample may be helpful. For this reason, the analysis attempted to quantify responses, and look for any noticeable variation in gender and age, as well as undertake more qualitative interpretation.

Lastly, it should be noted that variation also emerged in the way pupils responded to the interview questions. Some chose to elaborate on their own motivations for disaffected behaviour in considerable detail and dismiss causes outside their own experience. Others voiced their views by giving assent or dissent to each probe in turn (albeit sometimes fairly monosyllabically). Such variety of responses needs to be acknowledged during the quantification that follows. Above all, it is intended as a useful discussion point and not a definitive survey finding.

PART ONE
PUPILS' PERSPECTIVES ON THE CAUSES OF TRUANCY AND DISRUPTION

INTRODUCTION

This section of the report explores pupils' opinions on the main reasons for behaviour and attendance problems in school. Each youngster was invited to comment generally on each of these manifestations of disaffection and then, as follow-up, was also asked to respond to probes suggesting that causes might include friends, family, teachers, lessons and curriculum, or influences in the neighbourhood. This list of prompts mirrored the range of factors underpinning disaffection which were identified by educational professionals in Phase One of the project.

In response to the question of what they perceived to be the main causes of truancy and disruption, the pupil sample suggested (in rank order):

- **the influence of friends and peers**

- **relationships with teachers**

- **the content and delivery of the curriculum**

- **family factors**

- **bullying**

- **the classroom context (individual learning support and classroom management)**

- **problems arising from their own personality or learning abilities.**

For reference purposes, quantification of responses is given in full in the Appendix.

THE INFLUENCE OF FRIENDS AND PEERS

More than any other factor, the sample of 160 pupils nominated relations with peers and friends as a cause or stimulus for both truancy and disruption. Females - and in all three stages of schooling (KS2, KS3 and KS4) - referred to this most often.

One pupil perspective suggested that instigating disaffected behaviour was seen as a means of gaining kudos with peers, with sometimes an enjoyable 'buzz' from being the centre of attention, or being 'seen to be daring', also being a pay-off. This **status-** or **attention-seeking** perhaps confirms a pupil sub-culture which views anti-authority attitudes as an attractive aspiration or norm. It is worth noting that accounts which proposed a status-seeking motive for truancy were very much less common than for disruptive behaviour. Equally, the social insecurity underpinning attention-seeking behaviours came across in some of the interviews.

How pupils think peers affect ...	
... attendance	... behaviour
status-seeking	

It's daring [to truant] *with a friend, you really feel down in the dumps and can't be bothered with school, so* [truanting] *seems fun, a buzz.* (Female, Year 8)	*... you want people to think 'He shouted at a teacher'. Word gets around, you get big-headed ... People look at you, laugh, you want to make your friends laugh.* (Male, Year 10)
Some people say they're too tired to come to school and some say they can't be bothered ... they think they're being big and good and all that. (Male, Year 9)	*I came from a special school and I never knew anybody here, so I thought if I misbehave and show how good I am then people will want to make friends with me.* (Male, Year 10)
	It's attention seeking all the time, you know, 'Look at me, I'm hard, I can do whatever I want'. (Male, Year 10)
	I think if they've got friends and they think they're popular, then they like to do things what'll make them more popular - like X used to answer teachers back and things 'cos she thought 'Oh I'll look good if I do that'. (Female, Year 11)
	I used to just really show off ... to get me attention, 'cos I felt like alone, I just wanted people to, like, look at me and things like that, get attention off 'em all. (Male, Year 10)

However, other pupils' accounts actually offered a gradation of types of peer influence ranging from enticement to coercion. Thus, some interviewees recounted inducement by peers as an act of **joining in** with or imitating others' behaviour, and so providing a source of social fun or even a sense of solidarity or self-esteem (which outstripped the benefits of 'good' behaviour or attendance at school). Beyond that, involvement in disaffected behaviour was explained as a way of conforming to (or **blending in** with) peer expectations, thus averting possible teasing or harassment, or the threat of banishment from certain friendship groups.

How pupils think **peers** affect ...	
... attendance	**... behaviour**

joining in

Do you know, first it used to be all white I think and not much Asian boys. Now Asians are getting all into it, and it's not much people are coming to school, and it's getting like if one Asian knocks off, more and more go with them, you know, they all gang up. (Male, Year 9)	*[Friends] sort of join in together. Maybe they can't get on with the work ... something better to talk about like 'What are you doing after school?' or what they did the night before.* (Female, Year 11)
Say if your best friend's doing skiving off school, then you're going to want to do it as well so that you can hang around with them, 'cos you might not have any other friends at school . (Male, Year 10)	*If you think about the more corrupt of us, they certainly have a big effect on the people around. If someone's doing something, they're getting away with it and having a lot of fun, certainly it rubs off on you and you think, 'Oh, it'll be good for a laugh'.* (Male, Year 12)
Some people think if my mates can do it, I can do it, try to be like them, try to be big and hard - they don't want to feel left out and so do the same thing as what their friends do. (Female, Year 11)	*... if other people are messing about they'll probably do the same. If they're having fun and getting away with it.* (Male, Year 9)
Friends - if they're wagging it, you feel left out and just end up truanting. (Female, Year 10)	*There is a few lads in my science lesson and like one starts something off and the others are like laughing and they just all join in and they're encouraging them more then.* (Female, Year 10)

blending in

Sometimes people don't feel like [truanting] at all but they just do it 'cos of what their friends are going to say. (Female, Year 9)	*... if a friend's messing about and you're sat working, then you'll start messing about with them so you're not the only one working.* (Female, Year 10)

A further stage of the continuum of peer influence was the reporting of actual examples of teasing and **goading**. At the furthest extreme, outright **bullying** by peers was seen as the cause of some examples of attendance problems, while (albeit less often) retaliation to peer harassment was felt to account for some incidences of disruptive behaviour.

How pupils think peers affect ...	
... attendance	... behaviour

goading

Friends can tell you not to go [to school] *and go with them, but it's up to you, it's up to you to make up your mind - if you don't want to go you say 'No, I'm going to school', and then they call you 'goody two-shoes', and then you think 'I can't go to school 'cos everyone will start calling me names', so then you don't go.* (Female, Year 11)	*... if you get dared to do something, you might feel 'Ah well, all my friends are going to call me a* ['chicken'] *if I don't do it ... And as soon as they call you that, right, then everybody will start laughing ... and it's like your cheeks are going red and you're hot and you're all flustered ... so if I do it they're all going to be patting me on the back ...* (Female, Year 10)
... if you don't do what your friends say and stay off, they won't be your friends. (Female, Year 7)	*... if, like, someone's messing around and if you don't join in, they'll say, like, 'Oh look at him, look how good he is, he's a "goody-goody", and that.* (Male, Year 10)
	There's usually one person like [will start it] *and the others go ... 'Oh he's just pressed the self-destruction button, let's mess around, let's wind him up' 'cos it's like that one kid is the button and the others are just using him to go 'kaboom!'* (Male, Year 8)

bullying

[If you say no to truancy] *people tell other people and it gets around school, and the person gets left on their own with all people, like, bullying them.* (Female, Year 9)	*I think it's your friends, the way they influence you* [that leads to disruption], *because in our class there's a group of girls and they all hang around together, and they try and get you into trouble, and sometimes you have to follow them ... I think that's been my problem because I didn't want to keep in, I didn't want to get into trouble, and now they're bullying me because of it.* (Female, Year 8)
I didn't like school, and sometimes it was because of the other people cussing me or something, and getting me upset. I'd just say 'I'm not going' ... [Then] *I felt better because I knew I wouldn't get cussed and all that and get upset, so I thought it would be better if I stopped going to school - there's no-one to bother me.* (Male, Year 10)	*I got the hump because I was bullied at school, and had problems indoors, and I just couldn't handle none of it. So I just flipped out when I was at school ... I felt like I should've been dead, I shouldn't have been here at all, you feel right out of place and everyone's laughing at you.* (Female, Year 11)
I had a really bad home problem at the time, and a few people found out about it, and it went round the school, and I couldn't face going to school 'cos everyone took the mick and I couldn't handle going back in. (Female, Year 11)	*Kids wind me up - they call me names* [about my skin complaint] *and that, so I near enough go and hit 'em and when I do, I go and get a detention.* (Male, Year 8)

The strong perception by pupils that peer-related factors very often underpin disaffected behaviours raises a number of discussion points (although it is first worth revisiting the caveat about how far this response represents youngsters' general 'locus of control' problems, illustrating the characteristic of not being able to take responsibility for actions which is sometimes exhibited by disaffected pupils).

The fact that, in the view of pupils, **peers** dominate the list of factors influencing truancy, and especially disruptive behaviours, stands in marked contrast to the weight of opinion expressed by educational professionals as reported in the previous discussion paper *Three to Remember*. As such, it is perhaps not surprising that the audit of school-based strategies to combat disaffection did not often come across initiatives described as being specifically targeted at counteracting negative peer influence or subverting inappropriate friendship patterns (nor indeed harnessing peer culture to that end).

Clearly, initiatives such as peer mentors, and some examples of alternative or extra-curricular provision, may be said to provide a counterpoise to peer influence upon disaffected behaviour. Also, the befriending role of school counsellors, school-based educational welfare staff and so on may offer a kind of surrogate positive peer support, or act as facilitator for pupils to support each other. Equally, anti-bullying strategies, including those which offer specific assertiveness training and role play, might reflect a valuable approach for those pupils who feel themselves goaded or coerced into inappropriate attendance or behaviour patterns. Beyond that, separation from peers and friends was part of many school sanction systems, such as withdrawal units - and indeed was reported by pupils as the most painful part of any censure involving isolation or exclusion. Also relevant here may be the efficiency of a school's strategies for maintaining and monitoring attendance (which might thus pre-empt some peer-influenced or status-seeking truancy).

However, the significance of school-based initiatives which seek actively to counter or harness peer influence, as opposed to those with an emphasis on suppressing it, may be an important issue for those planning or evaluating work in this area. It perhaps also suggests that the curtailment of extra-curricular activities, which has been perceived by teachers as a consequence of the imperatives to emerge from the Education Reform Act, makes one further link between the National Curriculum and pupil disaffection. The resulting decrease in opportunities for the provision of supervised, purposeful and collaborative leisure activity among peers may be a particular loss.

FAMILY FACTORS

The sample, and notably the older (KS4) girls within it, provided a range of examples illustrating how they felt family and home background were an influence on both truancy and disruptive behaviour. Gender and age differences were more marked here, in that half of the 14 primary boys suggested family as a factor in behaviour, while the older boys, particularly KS4, mentioned family a lot less frequently. The high rating of family issues as a reason for non-attendance among females in KS4 (compared to KS3) is perhaps also worth noting.

By and large, pupils referred to parents and family influence in two distinct ways and both of these mirror closely factors which educational professionals had raised. Some pupils suggested home circumstances in effect authenticated attendance or behaviour patterns - examples of **parentally condoned absence** were described, and also what might be called '**parentally validated aggression**', both verbal and physical. This parental authentication was particularly evident among the primary sample. Other pupils proposed that truancy and disruptive conduct were a consequence of - or reaction to - **family problems**. In the light of home circumstances, some pupils found relating to peers or teachers either difficult or simply too daunting to attempt. In some instances, the severity of home factors was very apparent: divorce and separation, difficult relations with step-siblings or step-parents, bereavement, abuse, violence, and drug-taking within the family were all described. Equally, what appeared to be fairly average tensions and disagreements between parents and adolescent were also seen to trigger similar disaffected reactions.

How pupils think **family** affects ...	
... attendance	**... behaviour**

parental authentication

[People stay off school] *to go down town with mum and help her get some food; or if their dad's at work and their mum's ill, they have to go and help their mum and go to the shop for them.* (Female, Year 4)	*I've been brought up to ...* [fight], *'cos my dad's always been a hard person and he's built so ... and he's always wanted me like that but look at the size of me.* (Male, Year 9)
When I was younger ... I liked school but could never go 'cos I had to look after my brother and sister. (Male, Year 10)	*I've been told by my parents if somebody hits me I've got to hit them back, that's the way I've been brought up.* (Male, Year 7)
If people's parents were more strict they wouldn't bunk as much, because their mum would say something as well. But mum didn't really care, so I bunked, and she didn't say anything about it, just let the school sort it out. One day me and two of my mates bunked it. I went back to my house and my mum, she said 'Where have you been today?' and I said 'I didn't bother going' and she didn't say anything. My mate's mum whacked him round the head with a badminton racket, the other one got grounded for six months. Mum didn't say nothing really. (Male, Year 11)	*... if, like at home, people around them swear or things like that, I think* [kids will] *be more likely to swear at school.* (Male, Year 6) *I used to get bullied, they used to take my money off me and my dad says 'If I find you've had a fight and someone's hit you and you haven't hit them back, I'm gonna hit you'. Happened a couple of times and I thought 'I ain't taking this no more' so I started getting in with the big boys.* (Male, Year 8)

family problems

I didn't come to middle school 'cos I had lots of family problems, and my mum used to make me stay at home 'cos me dad, he used to hit her, and she said 'You'll have to stay at home in case he comes back', and I just stayed at home 'cos I felt right horrible if I came to school. (Female, Year 9)	[I was disruptive] *partly 'cos I was, like at home, frightened, frightened of my dad ... Now my dad's gone, it's a lot better.* (Male, Year 9)
There was a girl in my year, her mum and dad were splitting up, and she seemed to have a lot of time off. She used to stay at home because of the arguments but she used to go and just walk around places, feel as though she couldn't come to school. (Female, Year 11)	*You could have loads of problems on your mind, and everyone's getting on your nerves and you can't handle nothing, and you're just shouting at everyone all the time, and when you're in class and you can't concentrate, and people are getting on your nerves, you just get these blinkers and it just goes, then you just start going off the rails.* (Female, Year 10)
I had a lot of home problems and couldn't handle school. First it would be two days' bunking off a week, then it would be weeks, then it would be months. (Female, Year 11)	*My friend hardly sees her mum and dad. He's too tired, he works all night and sleeps all day and her mam's a cleaner so she's working all day. The only reason she's being naughty is to get attention in school 'cos she doesn't get enough at home.* (Female, Year 9)

Clearly, family influence raises a number of issues for school-based work, not least of which is the degree to which current pastoral provision can offer the kinds of support - and time - which youngsters with home-related problems may require. Systems to ensure home-school liaison, communication between staff on troubled pupils, and the management of children in stress may also be areas for consideration, and indeed funding. The merit of a sustained support role, such as school counsellor or school-based EWS staff, and also the use of multi-agency approaches, might be evident from these accounts. The value of intervention at primary-school level in order to break through parental authentication of inappropriate behaviour or attendance patterns may be highlighted here as well.

TEACHER/PUPIL INTER-RELATIONS

The problem of relating successfully with teachers as a cause of both classroom disruption and truancy was suggested by nearly half of the sample. Boys, and notably those in KS4, nominated teacher relationships as a factor in non-attendance more than girls; while KS3 and KS4 girls more often perceived a connection between disruptive behaviour and teacher relations.

Pupils' explanations clustered around three main 'problematic' teacher characteristics: demonstrations of **'lack of respect'** or consideration to pupils (a particular issue mentioned by KS4 boys in connection with non-attendance); a sense of **teacher injustice** about being unfairly blamed, singled out or excessively punished (noted especially by KS3 boys, or those who had left mainstream schooling at that stage); and, most simply, the volume and tone of teachers' voices, or what might be termed negative reactions to **teacher self-presentation**.

How pupils think **teacher-relations affect ...**	
... attendance	... behaviour

lack of respect

The teachers should talk to you like you're human, not like you're a monster or something ... if teachers weren't like that then more people would start going to school. (Female, Year 11) *It's the teachers that cause truancy - not so much the work 'cos the work's usually OK. The teachers' attitude to you, the way they talk down at you - they've got no right.* (Male, Year 11)	*It's the teachers' attitude to kids, that's the only reason people mess about ... I would be happy to do the work if they gave you it in the proper way, [instead] they're aggressive to you and trying to show their power off, that's all they do.* (Male, Year 11) *This teacher, she treats us like we're tiny infants ... it hurts 'cos I know I shouldn't say some of the things I say but it hurts also 'cos some of the things she says upsets me as well.* (Female, Year 10)

teacher injustice

Sometimes kids get wronged by their teachers when they shouldn't be - it isn't their fault but they still get wronged - so people don't come [to school]. (Male, Year 7) *The teachers didn't like me and I didn't like them, they didn't understand me. If something went wrong, they used to say it was me, most of the time I used to say 'Yes, it was me' 'cos I didn't like grassing at all. I felt lousy most of the time, I was like thinking none of the teachers liked me and I can't talk to no-one.* (Male, Year 10) *If all the class does something wrong, but just one person gets the blame, and they haven't done it, so then they don't go* [to school]. (Male, Year 9)	*Every teacher has a bad impression of me - none of them like us. Even if they haven't taught us before, and say I was walking around and wasn't doing anything wrong, they just take it out on me - if something went wrong further down the corridor and they see me, they get me in the office and give me a detention or something.* (Male, Year 9) *It would be easier to behave if things were more fair, but most of the time the teachers aren't fair, you either sit there and take it like an idiot, or you stick up for yourself.* (Female, Year 10) *The teacher wasn't treating me fairly, she was shouting and if you're having a bad day and they start shouting at you, getting you into trouble, the teacher shouting again ... you just flip ...* (Male, Year 10)

teacher self-presentation	
*The teachers who shout, if people don't like it, they just wag that lesson, 'cos some teachers **talk** to you when they tell you to be good, others just shout at you, so you don't listen to them.* (Male, Year 9)	*I like Miss Y, the music teacher, but sometimes like when I'm getting the keyboards out, right, I forget which socket to plug it in ... and then she realises it's wrong and she really shouts in your ear. It makes me angry and I go to Miss 'How come you're telling me off all the time?', and she just tells me to shut up and stuff.* (Female, Year 7)
Sometimes, when I didn't go to school I used to not come because the teachers were always getting on at me ... it felt you just come to school to get done all the time ... Mr X was always shouting at me. (Female, Year 9)	*Last year I was scared of one of my maths teachers and I didn't know what to do and I was too frightened to ask for any help just in case he'd shout at me 'cos that's what he was like. So you just sit there and talk to your friends and get them in trouble and get yourself in trouble.* (Female, Year 11)
Some of the teachers have deep voices and it scares people and they don't come. (Male, Year 10)	
Kids stay away, 'cos the teachers, even a normal teaching teacher, they're walking around, like they're the headmaster picking and poking at everyone. If one teacher is in a bad mood, all of them are in a bad mood and then they get all the students in a bad mood ... (Female, Year 11)	*A lot of people mess about just because of the teachers, or to get on the teacher's nerves. If the teacher's shouting at everyone, everyone will mess about to get on their nerves even more.* (Female, Year 10)
The teachers get on kids' nerves and stuff like that, the teachers being just stroppy really, always being horrible and shouting - the kids might just want to get away from the class. (Male, Year 7)	

Clearly, interpreting these findings requires much caution, for logically the thrust of this pupil viewpoint might be said to confuse the consequence of misconduct (i.e. teacher displeasure or control techniques) with the original cause of that displeasure (i.e. transgression of rules concerning acceptable behaviour). Perhaps the most valuable way to consider such assertions about these pupil-teacher tensions is to see them as 'scripts' or verbal 'repertoires' which indicate or presage disaffection and a systemic breakdown between pupil and school. Indeed, those pupils interviewed in off-site provision often voiced a script of universal discrimination, with antagonism to school and teachers in general, when they described the events and emotions leading up to their exit from mainstream school.

A major challenge for schools may therefore be to consider strategies - whether pastoral or curricular - which can reverse or prevent these pupil perceptions and their accompanying problematic attitudes and behaviours. Does staff training or discussion in areas such as conflict management and consistency in sanctions have a place here? It might be worth noting that pupils' accounts suggest that systemic breakdown is often a slow and gradual process, and that many of those disaffected youngsters still in school volunteered descriptions of individual teachers' positive qualities, including empathy and inter-personal skills, humour and 'good' classroom control.

Recognising that there may be distinctive teacher behaviours and qualities which are particularly appropriate for managing difficult or disaffected pupils (and conversely some which are very inappropriate) could be an important component of a school's strategic thinking in the area of disaffection. Providing opportunities for such special skills to be used with disengaged youngsters within a school's learning context and also pastoral/social situations may be another issue, though ultimately, of course, one of resource priorities.

CURRICULUM AND THE CLASSROOM

Another aspect of school life which the sample suggested as a factor in causing disaffected behaviours involved either the **curriculum content** (including certain types of learning activities) or the **classroom context** in which this curriculum was delivered (pupils citing classroom management/control and differentiation issues).

It was particularly noticeable that 'uninteresting' lessons or 'being bored with work' ranked as a reason for truancy more often than disruption by all the sub-samples. KS3 boys and girls gave a higher number of references to lessons as a reason for both attendance and classroom behaviour difficulties. While lessons featured minimally among the girls at primary school as having any association with disaffected behaviours, six of the 14 primary school boys also suggested a link between non-attendance and lesson content. KS4 boys and girls, by comparison, rated lessons as a factor in truancy and disruption considerably below the influence of peers and teacher relations. This variation raises at least the possibility that, for some children, there is a sequence of disaffection and alienation which has its origins in non-motivating encounters with learning activities and curriculum content much before the KS4 watershed.

However, it should be noted that a number of the secondary-aged youngsters who cited boredom as the only reason for non-attendance also volunteered that this would result in truanting from specific lessons, rather than missing a full day.

Pupils' fuller explanations of 'boredom' often related to specific **learning tasks** which they were required to do in lessons, and the lack of variety within these. Perhaps not surprisingly, constant writing and copying tasks received most criticism, while positive comment was particularly made about practical/experimental work, design- or IT-related activities and opportunities to work collaboratively.

How pupils think the **curriculum** affects ...	
... attendance	**... behaviour**
learning tasks	
If you like [have to] *do writing today, you make yourself sick and you say 'Mum, I'm sick'. Then she might let you have the day off school ... a lot of people don't like writing in our class.* (Male, Year 5)	[The main reason for disruption is] *the school curriculum, it's so boring. We just have to sit down, do writing all the time.* [We should do] *more practical work like in history, going to museums or something;* [in maths] *actually using the things that's in the books, like calculators.* (Male, Year 9)
I don't think the lessons have got a lot to do with [whole day truancy], *like sometimes, I've just bunked off lessons 'cos I've thought 'Oh God it's science and I don't wanna do science', and just go to the toilets for however long the lesson is, but if you're bunking off a whole day it's* **not** *'cos of the lessons, it's 'cos you've got a problem.* (Female, Year 10)	*Last time* [I was disruptive] *was in cooking ...'cos that day we weren't cooking, just writing. It was boring.* (Female, Year 9)
Boredom and not being good at lessons [causes truancy], *they've no interest in work, like I'm no good at writing and stuff, I don't like that sort of thing, but it's all that, all the way through school.* (Male, Year 9)	[When I misbehave] *I'm just bored usually, 'cos in German on a Thursday we're in the language lab and we're usually listening to tapes and it's just really boring just sat there.* (Male, Year 8)
There's nothing to look forward to coming to school - the teacher just sits and reads it out to you, they should make lessons more exciting. (Female, Year 10)	*It's boredom, if you're bored in a lesson you ain't going to just sit there, you're going to muck around 'cos there's nothing else to do ... just sitting in a room and being talked at ain't all that pleasant.* (Female, Year 10)

Rather than any specific learning tasks within the lesson, other features of the curriculum in the classroom which pupils linked to disaffected behaviour included the **lack of relevance** or interest in the lesson's overall content, and also the **lack of stimulus** and subject accessibility in some of the teaching they received.

How pupils think the **curriculum** affects ...	
... attendance	... behaviour
lack of relevance	
[I truanted from lessons because] *I thought it was boring and I didn't really need to know anything about it, right, 'cos if I were going for a job they wouldn't ask you about that certain stuff.* (Male, Year 10)	*I don't like English, it's just that they do Shakespeare and that and I don't like Shakespeare ... in English I don't pay much attention to it, I just talk most of the time.* (Female, Year 9)
lack of stimulus	
*It's the subject, they don't do anything **interesting,** like you just can't be bothered going in and sitting down in a room and not doing anything. It's not the teachers, it's the lessons.* (Female, Year 10) *When it's boring, then you don't really want to go ... you think 'God I'm not going to sit there ... '* (Female, Year 10) *I think with some of the lessons, like physics, a lot of people don't understand it, and don't want to come. I think that the teacher doesn't explain it very well ... a lot of people have problems with Mr X, it's always 'Oh no, we've got physics now'. I think Mr X seems to think he knows it, and **tells** you everything, he thinks 'Well I know it, they must understand it'. But I think he's a bit or very proud of what he does, and it wouldn't seem right to him to go and sort of explain it to everybody.* (Male, Year 11)	*... if you find a lesson boring then you do tend to mess about and not take notice of the work, so teachers should try and make it a lot more exciting than it is. I mean there are some lessons which you can't but they should at least try - to get the people into it.* (Female, Year 10) *You come in the lesson and it's like they've got what they're going to teach you and they just read out what you're going to achieve, and they're chatting a whole load of nonsense, and you're not understanding a word they're saying, and they're just using these big words and everything, and you're sitting there and you're bored, so then you start chatting to your friend ...* (Female, Year 10) *I* [misbehave] *'cos of the boring lessons, you want to liven things up a bit.* (Male, Year 9)

Many of these responses may reflect the 'disenfranchisement' from an appropriate curriculum which was referenced by educational professionals and reported in *Three to Remember*. However, perhaps not surprisingly, pupils' reasons for disengagement invariably focused upon the mediation of that curriculum by their teachers, rather than upon any national prescriptions on the content of learning. Significantly, some schools were encouraging their subject departments to reconsider the variety of learning tasks made available to pupils as part of their strategies to deal with pupil disaffection.

While some pupils focused on learning tasks and curriculum content, others made references to teacher management of the learning environment as a source of disaffection. Here two major issues emerged: the way teachers were perceived to address **individuals' learning needs** and how effectively they maintained **control and discipline**. On both these classroom context aspects, the sample suggested a link with disruption more often than truancy, which might suggest that if pupil dissatisfaction focuses specifically on the inadequacy of the *learning* relationship with their teacher, it is more likely to stimulate militant rather than evasive action. This was particularly the case when control and discipline was the factor under discussion, although examples of non-attendance because of classroom control issues were offered.

How pupils think the **classroom context affects ...**	
... attendance	... behaviour
control and discipline	
Some people if they're in a class where nobody's working 'cos the teacher is weak, then they'll think 'Oh I've got that lesson today but nobody works and I can't work so I may as well stay off'. (Female, Year 11)	*Some teachers can't control the class and that's a good chance to mess about. (Female, Year 9)*
	We can't just like let teachers shout at us all the time, they think we get on with our work if they like shout as us, but we don't 'cos we get on with our work if we've got a canny teacher. (Male, Year 10)

However, the sense that teachers were failing to provide appropriate learning support for them as individuals - i.e. the whole issue of differentiation - emerged as a very strong factor for pupils in both disruption and truancy. Accounts from some pupils conveyed a sense of painful frustration because they felt they were being made to wait for assistance, being ignored or having their learning difficulties publicly exposed.

How pupils think the **classroom context affects ...**	
... attendance	... behaviour
individual learning needs	
When I didn't understand a bit of work, the teachers never used to bother ... so I thought, 'Sod it, if they ain't gonna help me, I ain't gonna help meself, I'm not going to school'. (Male, Year 10)	*Sometimes like ... when I'm in Mr X's class and I say 'Sir, can you help me?' and he's chatting away, and he says 'I'll be there in two minutes', and he goes round helping other kids and I say 'You ain't helped me yet', and he says 'Wait', and then the bell goes for my next lesson - that's when I get really, extremely angry.* (Female, Year 7)
I used to go to my teacher 'Miss, I don't understand this', and she'd say 'Go sit down and read it', and you'd go back up to her again and she'd say 'Read it properly', and it's like I'd just read it or tried to read it anyway ... 'What can't you read?' - then she shouts it out loud and everyone starts to take the mickey out of you. So if teachers weren't like that more people would start going to school. (Female, Year 11)	*If I didn't understand the work I'd get, like, in a temper. I'd just mess about or close me eyes and shut meself off, like, and not listen to what anyone said. I'd get, like, really aggressive ... I used to understand perfect, just when I got up here it seemed, like, new to me - French and all that. Like, I couldn't read, like you had to read from a book, and I couldn't do it, so I used to chuck the book away, or chuck it at a kid or summat.* (Male, Year 10)
My friend was scared to come to school 'cos he might've felt stupid to get it wrong in front of his mates. (Male, Year 8)	
[I dogged it 'cos] the school was too big ... like it was so many in the class ... when I was there I used to get stuck and all that. Instead of putting my hand up for some help I used to just sit there and I used to get stressed out with myself 'cos I couldn't do it and everyone else was like working and doing it and I was just sat there thinking to myself, 'What's the matter with me, why can't I do it?'. (Male, Year 11)	*Most of the time [you misbehave] because you're bored to death, and can't understand a single thing the teacher's doing. You can ask them for help but they make you look stupid. They say 'I've explained it so many times, you should have been paying attention', but they're not speaking in a way that you can understand. You get bored and think that the teacher just makes me look stupid, so I might as well cause trouble.* (Female, Year 10)
If I was learning something, and the teachers would help me, and treat me like a normal person instead of just sending me out and that I think I would've been all right, but once that started happening I just couldn't see the point [of coming to school]. (Male, Year 10)	*[In science I misbehave] 'cos I have difficulty ... he sets you some work and I don't understand it, and I put my hand up and he comes over and says things but I don't even understand them, then he goes away, and I keep putting my hand up but he just walks straight past us.* (Male, Year 10)

Clearly, embedded in some of these accounts is a range of deeper problems for the pupil and his/her school to 'own' and resolve, including managing anger, general attitudes to learning or teacher-relations, and the downward-spiralling consequences of falling behind with school work through non-attendance (or inattention). However, it does once more place the experience of the curriculum, and particularly how schools and teachers mediate that experience, as a central issue in disaffection. Many of these youngsters' accounts featured the viewpoint that their particular learning needs were neither being fully appreciated nor properly responded to.

It is no surprise that a number of schools and LEAs in the sample are indeed focusing upon curriculum, and particularly differentiation and individual learning needs, as a key component of their strategies for improving behaviour and attendance.

PART TWO
THE EXPERIENCE OF DISAFFECTION

This section of the report looks briefly at the sample's personal accounts of the experiences and also the emotions surrounding disaffected behaviour. The wide range of factors which may influence and underpin pupil disaffection has been covered many times, in a number of important research studies, as well as in the present report and its sister publication *Three to Remember*. How it actually feels to be disaffected perhaps has been given less attention. Offering the testaments that follow is a small attempt towards redressing this.

From the interviews, three powerful affective feelings consistently emerged: put simply, disaffected pupils described themselves as mostly **bored,** often **angry**, and sometimes **frightened.** Of course, how the youngster handled - or perhaps more accurately, *mishandled* - that boredom, anger or fear varied, as did the severity of the problems underpinning these feelings.

However, the sample's accounts suggest that it is possible to see truancy and disruptive behaviour as alternative strategies (evasion or confrontation) to resolve a similar range of emotional discomfort. In the notable phrase of one Principal Welfare Officer, attendance and behaviour difficulties represent **flight or fight** options.

BOREDOM

a yawn is a silent shout ... (G. K. Chesterton, 1874-1936)

The descriptor 'boredom' surfaced inexorably throughout the interviews. As exemplified in the previous section, school and the curriculum encountered there were often portrayed by disaffected pupils as an essentially unstimulating experience, triggering disruptive behaviour or non-attendance. Yet the act of truancy itself was usually also depicted as dull and not a little unnerving. A very few interviewees did recall their truancy in fairly positive terms, describing adventurous and sociable outings to parks, bomb-sites, golf links, shopping centres, 'safe' houses in the vicinity, or trips on public transport. However, the majority actually depicted truancy as a furtive, lonely experience, providing very little pleasure or stimulus:

> [truanting] *is a bit boring, you're scared all the time that someone goes past and sees you.*

> *There's nothing to do, you just go to a cafe, sitting down, it's boring. I used to think I wish I was back in school because at least there's something to do - there you're just watching people playing snooker, playing arcade machines and that's it.*

> *Well truanting weren't as good as all that 'cos you don't have much fun. You're too scared that you might see someone you know, there's too much fear than being able to enjoy yourself, you're better off staying in lessons.*

> *It's boring having the day off, hiding all the time ... it is boring out there.*

> *It feels like weird 'cos you knocks off and you're thinking like you'll get caught - I didn't enjoy it ... the first time I was fretting, but when I did it I wasn't as nervous as I was the first time - but now I think it was a mistake.*

> *I used to stay in most of the time, watching telly and just mucking about but after a while it gets boring, nothing to do, same thing everyday, and you miss your friends.*

Deception of parents and school was sometimes mentioned as part of truanting procedures: forging notes or making fake phone-calls to school registration administrators; intercepting written communication from school to parents; returning home once parents had left for work; inventing dentist appointments to neighbours or relatives; taking other clothes to change into and so on.

Likewise, children who operated post-registration truancy strategies described a number of ploys to avoid encountering boring or discomforting lessons. Hiding within earshot of the school bell in order to attend later lessons was fairly common: in toilets, behind playground walls, in under-used parts of the school (e.g. drama and computer rooms or out-of-the-way staircases) were all mentioned. More adventurous approaches involved exploiting very public visibility, such as sitting in prominent places and claiming appointments with other staff, or blending in with an audience watching play rehearsals, sports lessons or fixtures.

It may be ironic that the enterprise, ingenuity and risk-taking involved in lesson evasion could not be channelled into those very curriculum experiences which the youngsters were so resolved to avoid.

Boredom was also linked directly to disaffected behaviour within school. Some pupils described their disruptiveness in class as a considered choice, to provide an alternative source of interest, with such typical comments as '*Being bored in the lesson - you just have to try and have a laugh when you're in there*' or '*Shouting out and joking makes the lesson go faster, 'cos it's boring not talking*'. In other instances, the disruptive behaviour was explained as almost an inadvertent or compulsive reaction to lack of stimulus: '*I just get bored with the work, and then I just get carried away*'.

Of course, 'boredom' here can be seen as another sort of script or verbal repertoire, masking (or acting as metaphor for) a wide range of learning problems, such as special educational needs; difficulties in application; concentration problems. Nevertheless, the script of 'boredom' voiced by the sample does once more confirm curriculum dislocation as a central feature of disaffected pupils' school lives.

ANGER

> *Anger is a kind of temporary madness ...* (Saint Basil, 330-379)

Many of the pupil interviewees described feeling angry as a precursor or component of their disaffected behaviour. The source of that anger was described as either home-induced (and so brought into school) or directly triggered by situations encountered there. For some, this anger was explained as a desperately difficult emotion to handle, with the resulting behaviour largely compulsive and uncontrollable.

> *I do it all the time, I can't help it, arguing and shouting, swearing at teachers - I get in a bad temper and freak out, I just feel like punching someone.*

> *If you're having a bad day and start getting into trouble and a teacher shouts at you, and you just flip ... sometimes if I'm feeling bad, I just go mental, I don't know what to do about it ...*

> *The teachers or kids are getting on your nerves - if I'm going to behave badly, I'm going to behave badly - there's no way of stopping it.*

> *When I'm in an eggy mood and that, I just retaliate, and, if the teacher has a go at me, I say 'Just go away' and all that. When they say 'Minus mark', I say 'I don't effing care' - sometimes I feel so angry inside ...*

Other pupils described walking out of their classroom in a state of emotional turmoil.

> *Some of the time, I had like mass arguments with the teachers and everything and just walked out.*

There were also examples of pupils explaining how evasion of school situations where such anger and aggression might flair up was a more considered strategy:

> *One of my mates always truants because this guy used to humiliate him in lessons, all the time. He can't stand that, he's got a short temper, 'cos he knows he'll just end up fighting and he knows if he fights in the lesson, he'll get excluded, so he stays away.*

> *When I'm bunking off school, you feel like 'I should be in school', but when you're bunking off, you feel more calm because you don't have the stress of people getting on your nerves or teachers nagging you - so you feel more calm and more settled and you're peaceful instead of being so hysterical inside and everything.*

For others, anger was depicted as the impetus underpinning more deliberate anti-school reactions.

> *I got annoyed by a teacher - I just kept arguing with her, if they told me to do something, I'd just ignore them and not do my work - I was cross - 'cos they did like to show you up in front of the class and that, that's why I just ignored them, to try and get my own back.*

> *Those who have grievances, and nothing's done about it, they start acting up in class, and that's when the trouble starts ...*

Within all these accounts is no doubt an issue of children learning to manage their own behaviour, as well as staff expertise and school procedures in dealing with - or diffusing - such outbursts. The prevalence of 'anger' across the sample may perhaps usefully raise the profile of this problem and remove it from being regarded as a stigma or personal failure by individual teachers.

FEAR

> *No passion so effectively robs the mind of all its powers of acting and reasoning as fear ...* (Edmund Burke, 1729-1797)

Fear was another emotion which surfaced regularly among the pupils' accounts of disaffected behaviour. Not surprisingly, where youngsters suggested they were frightened, it had usually triggered evasion and hence blanket non-attendance. Bullying by other pupils was most often pinpointed as a source of fear, though actually a youngster's difficult home circumstances or learning ability might be intrinsically linked to the harassment. Whatever its origins, some of the descriptions graphically registered the depth of anxiety experienced:

> *I had school phobia, partly 'cos I was bullied ... there was this long road to school and from the top like, I could see my school and the closer I got, the building just seemed to get much bigger and bigger and I felt 'No, I just can't go in there'.*

> *I mean this boy was bullying me, from as soon as I stepped out of my house and into the road, that's what it felt like. You know I was going 'Oh God, I've got another day with him in my class' so I bunked off.*

> *I just got bullied, and it was like being trapped in a box with spiders. Basically, you wanna get out, but you can't ... just the thought of that school [still] gives me the shakes.*

> *They find anything about me and they tease me for it. If they feel like picking on someone, it's usually me first ... every now and then, my lunch sort of disappears, but I get it back when the bell's about to go. So sometimes I stuff it in my pocket and eat it between lessons, not in them though ... they have a habit of going in my bag and taking things out, throwing them around the class but that's only in certain lessons, with certain teachers.*

Bullying is of course a specialist area in its own right, in receipt of focused school or LEA GEST initiatives, as well as large-scale research programmes. As Part One has shown, fearful **anticipation** of harassment (or exclusion from friendship groups) if they failed to conform to peer expectation was also an experience mentioned by some of the sample.

The significance of all this for the present research project (and its broad-ranging focus on positive strategies by schools) needs to be stressed. Being afraid of peers, or rather the physical and psychological strength of peer culture, came across as a very clear emotion within this wide-ranging sample of disaffected pupils. However, references to fear of teachers - or the sanctions they could employ - were very much less common. Sometimes, but still rarely, pupils described the fear or anxiety attached to exposure of their work performance (tests, incompleted homework, etc.). In contrast to this, fear of parental sanctions or reactions which disaffected behaviour might induce did surface more regularly.

Anxiety about parental responses was, for some pupils, a significant deterrent, or sometimes was described as a factor in any contrition and reform. This fear was more often an issue in relation to truancy than disruption in school, no doubt because of the legal ramifications of non-attendance. Equally, parental sanctions cited by pupils (loss of pocket money, grounding, confiscation, physical reprimands) often had a clear and more direct 'hurt factor', which the youngsters acknowledged.

> *I know that if I get caught wagging it, or something, I'd get done dead bad at home - get grounded and probably get hit and all.*

> *Dad was reading the reports and it said that I was truancing and he goes 'What are you truancing for?' I goes 'I don't know dad, I just done it' and he goes 'Well you're grounded'. I goes 'No dad I didn't mean it'. He goes 'Get out then, don't do it again 'cos if you does it again you're grounded for three months'. So I've not done it since.*

> *The only person who encourages me to behave or anything like that is my mum, and I mean BEHAVE ...*

In comparison, for a number of this sample of disaffected pupils, mainstream school sanctions appeared as fairly impotent forms of censure.

> *Teachers can't really do owt can they - they could tell parents which puts a lot of people off ...*

> *Sometimes we get a break detention or a dinner detention but that doesn't stop us - it's just not, I dunno, we're not that bothered about detentions.*

Perhaps this confirms how vital additional strategies and resources are if pupil disengagement is to be properly addressed. The need for sustained financing to develop and maintain the targeted support systems already under way in schools is clearly evident, when problematic behaviour has not only such complex causes but also such intense emotions surrounding it.

This final section of the report looks at pupils' views on reducing disaffection. It was hoped that suggestions here might provide further insight into the factors underpinning disaffected behaviour, as well as offer insights into where the focus of remediating strategies could usefully lie.

The interview was structured so that after recounting personal experiences of truancy and disruption, and offering opinion on causes, each youngster was invited to suggest ways of encouraging better behaviour and attendance in school. Significantly, some children used this general question as an opportunity to talk about their own way of coming to terms with disaffection, and it is a selection of these accounts which will form the conclusion of the present paper.

First, however, rough quantification of the whole sample's responses showed the four top-ranking solutions overall revolved around:

> **curriculum content;**
> **teacher characteristics;**
> **school rewards and sanctions; or**
> **parental involvement.**

Again there was some notable variation according to the pupils' gender and age.

Thus, the highest ranking suggestion referred to some aspect of **curriculum content:** the sample as a whole stressed that lessons could offer more interest, more practical activities, more choice, more variety, more engagement with the real world (e.g. trips). Males, and particularly those in KS4, gave this category of response, and overall it was raised as a solution to truancy rather more often than as a way for addressing disruptive behaviour. Compared with the KS4 female responses, KS3 girls were more likely to mention a different curriculum as a way of improving disaffection.

The gender variation is noteworthy, offering some corroboration that curriculum disengagement has particular resonances for boys.

Teacher characteristics most commonly clustered around the issue of pupil-teacher relationships. It was often suggested that staff could '*talk to ...*' or '*treat ...*' pupils '*... differently*'. Expansions upon this difference included showing more justice, patience, understanding, respect, as well as humour and informality (though being 'more strict' surfaced occasionally and one pupil did suggest the solution to disaffection was that teachers should be taller).

Changing schools' **rewards and punishments** was also raised, though this was more often a lower school proposal. For sanctions, the suggestion was almost invariably that these should be stricter, while any rewards proposed usually involved outings, money, food or youth-culture consumer items. No doubt, this KS3 focus on extrinsic incentives and deterrents reflects a variation in maturity, and it may be an issue for schools to consider how - or if - their reward systems particularly match this difference in outlook. As a way of increasing the *gravitas* of the offence, **parental involvement** or informing parents was also regularly raised as a way of improving especially attendance, but also behaviour. Such findings particularly highlight the problem of what might constitute effective reprimands and deterrents for those pupils who have little regard for parental and school authority.

Beyond these four major areas, a few pupils focused on improvements to the **learning context**, with suggestions for: smaller classes, shorter lessons, teachers 'helping' more with the work, or simply '*better teaching*'. Others referred to the value of additional **pastoral support**: having '*someone to talk to*', a Childline, and a counsellor were all mentioned. Linked to this, a few pupils mentioned *smaller schools*, implying their current school ethos had resulted in some sense of unattachment or alienation. Another set of issues raised with some regularity related to the tensions between the visual symbols of school authority and those of youth culture: the institution's attitudes to certain types of clothing, jewellery, hairstyles (and also smoking) were all offered as areas where greater leniency would encourage better attendance and behaviour. Comments like these can be interpreted as the viewpoints of those youngsters who have not learned to recognise the appropriate way to play the role of pupil, or represent another version of the script of 'systemic breakdown' between the youngster and his/her school ethos. Rehabilitation or preventing this breakdown remains the key issue for strategies to deal with disaffection.

For this reason, the analysis looked closely at the narratives and viewpoints of those children who exemplified some noticeable reversal of disaffected attitudes, as it is these pupils' perspectives which may particularly signal appropriate strategies of support.

The accounts and ways of resolving disaffection which were offered by 'rehabilitated' children often tended to have one or more of three main elements that made them stand apart from others in the sample:

(i)   **they had begun to express the value and significance of education;**

(ii)   **they could recognise their own role and responsibility for their disaffected behaviour; or**

(iii)   **they were internalising parental - and sometimes their school's - disappointment and displeasure as something they wished to reverse.**

It is some of these testaments which will conclude the present report. However, it is important to stress that each of these pupil's recovery-statements was underpinned by some form of intensive and individuated support from their school or off-site unit. The focus of that support had involved providing alternative curriculum experiences or learning contexts, and/or pastoral work for behavioural or emotional problems. As a conclusion to solutions for disaffection, this suggests that there are considerable resource implications in any serious attempt to address pupils' disengagement from school, and yet, when such resources are available, the dedication and skill of educational professionals can produce highly positive outcomes.

I just got to thinking, like, when I gotta go towards my exams, and if I carries on like I have been I'll get terrible grades, I won't get to college, and [now] *I want to be a carpenter.*

You need to tell people what's going to happen to 'em if they don't come to school - like you're going to fail, you're going to do this, it's going to look really bad ... but you've got to drill it into their brains so they really understand.

I used to get hassled a lot by teachers, they always used to shout at me, bring my parents in. I'd go to school for a week, then I'd truant when I had the teacher who got me into trouble. Then I had advice, not told off, just talked to one-to-one ... then when I considered it, I realised there's no point. At the end of the day, teachers get their pay cheques - if we don't come, they don't lose anything, we're the ones who lose out. I've discovered my work is important. My parents expect a lot of me and I've only got a year left ... before I use to hate teachers, until I got talked to and that, and decided teachers aren't against you.

I used to think fighting solved everything, but now I think fighting solves nothing at all, it doesn't solve anything, messing about. I learnt the difficult way.

They said to me the whole school was disrupting, through one person the whole school was disrupting. I didn't like men, I didn't get on with the men teachers at all, and that's where my problems came from ... I didn't believe that men could tell me what to do. But I get on with men teachers now.

I'm not an angel now, but I used to be really bad ... I used to be arguing - I got bullied at first, 'cos I was short, then I started hanging around with the wrong people, smoking, and then I started fighting a lot. Then people used to start on me. I just tells myself now there's no point in looking for trouble 'cos you gotta grow up sometime and get a job - time goes quickly doesn't it ...?

I realised I went too far, that I shouldn't have done those things - it makes you realise a lot of things you shouldn't have done and you look back and say 'Why did I do it?' ... I was just being stupid, though I thought I was being clever.

I wasn't bothered 'cos I'd always wanted to fight this girl right bad, so I didn't really feel anything at all - I felt 'Yeah I've done it' - then I thought of my mum and that, it's not fair on them, is it? ... [exclusion] *made a lot of difference. It made me realise fighting isn't everything, and ... you mustn't misbehave, 'cos it all lingers over you.*

REFERENCES

CHAPLAIN, R. (1996). 'Making a strategic withdrawal: disengagement and self-worth protection in male pupils.' In Ruddock, J., Chaplain, R. and Wallace, G. (Eds). *School Improvement: What Can Pupils Tell Us?* London: David Fulton Publishers.

DAVIE, R. and GALLOWAY, D. (Eds) (1996). *Listening to Children in Education.* London: David Fulton Publishers.

GRAY, J. and JESSON, D. (1990). *Truancy in Secondary Schools Amongst Fifth-Year Pupils (Revised Version).* Sheffield: Sheffield University, Educational Research Centre.

ILEA (1984). *Improving Secondary Schools: Report of the Committee on Curriculum and Organisation of Secondary Schools* (Hargreaves Report). London: ILEA.

KINDER, K., HARLAND, J., WILKIN A., and WAKEFIELD, A. (1995). *Three to Remember: Strategies for Disaffected Pupils:* Slough: NFER.

LEARMONTH, J. (1995). *More Willingly to School? An Independent Evaluation of the DFEE's Truancy and Disaffected Pupils (TDP) GEST Programme.* London: DFEE.

RUDDOCK, J., CHAPLAIN, R. and WALLACE, G. (eds) *School Improvement: What Can Pupils Tell Us?* London: David Fulton Publishers.

STOLL, P. and O'KEEFE, D. (1989). *Officially Present: an Investigation into Post Registration Truancy in Nine Maintained Secondary Schools.* London: Institute of Economic Affairs.

APPENDIX

PUPILS' VIEWS ON THE CAUSES OF TRUANCY AND DISRUPTION

TRUANCY											
Males						**Females**					
Primary School N=14		**Lower School N=48**		**Upper School N=30**		**Primary School N=9**		**Lower School N=28**		**Upper School N=31**	
Bullying	6	Lessons	34	Teachers	23	Bullying	5	Peers	18	Peers	24
Teachers	6	Peers	31	Peers	20	Teachers	4	Lessons	18	Family	24
Family	6	Teachers	25	Lessons	15	Family	3	Teachers	14	Lessons	20
Lessons	6	Family	14	Family	14	Peers	3	Bullying	13	Bullying	18
Peers	3	Bullying	12	Bullying	12	Lessons	1	Family	11	Teachers	16
CC:ILN*	1	CC:ILN*	2	CC:ILN*	4	CC:ILN*	1	CC:ILN*	1	CC:ILN*	2

DISRUPTION											
Males						**Females**					
Primary School N=14		**Lower School N=48**		**Upper School N=30**		**Primary School N=9**		**Lower School N=28**		**Upper School N=31**	
Peers	10	Peers	35	Peers	18	Peers	6	Peers	21	Peers	24
Family	7	Lessons	19	Teachers	14	Bullying	3	Lessons	16	Family	19
Teachers	4	Teachers	18	Lessons	12	Teachers	1	Family	15	Teachers	17
Bullying	1	Family	12	CC:Control**	8	Lessons	1	Teachers	14	Lessons	12
Lessons	1	Bullying	4	Family	7			CC:Control**	6	Bullying	3
CC:ILN*	1	CC:ILN*	4	CC:ILN*	5			CC:ILN*	5	CC:ILN*	3
		CC:Control**	4	Bullying	4			Bullying	4	CC:Control**	3

*   Classroom Context: Individual Learning Needs
**   Classroom Context: Control

Note: The responses given are presented numerically rather than in percentage form. Interviewees could give more than one response.

PUPIL PERCEPTIONS OF DISAFFECTION:
a summary

disaffection **is caused by** ... (in rank order)

INFLUENCE OF PEERS	• status-seeking • joining in/blending-in • teasing/goading
RELATIONSHIPS WITH TEACHERS	• lack of respect to pupils • teacher injustice • teacher self-presentation
CURRICULUM CONTENT	• lack of relevance • lack of stimulus • lack of variety in learning task(s)
FAMILY FACTORS	• parental authentication • family problems
BULLYING	
CLASSROOM CONTEXT	• inadequate control and discipline • unaddressed individual learning needs

---

disaffection **is experienced as** ...

BOREDOM **ANGER** **FEAR**

---

disaffection **could be improved by changing** ... (in rank order)

• **curriculum content**
• **teacher characteristics**
• **rewards and sanctions**
• **parental involvement**

PUPIL PERCEPTIONS OF DISAFFECTION:
issues and implications

Countering negative **peer influence** may involve considering:

- the role of peer mentors

- alternative or extra curricular provision (especially collaborative work)

- specialist school-based staff offering a befriending role and/or facilitating peer support

- anti-bullying initiatives including assertiveness techniques

- the efficiency and profile of strategies for monitoring attendance

Issues

- *How far do school-based initiatives focus on harnessing peer culture and influence, rather than only suppressing it?*

- *What are the links between the curtailment of extra-curricular activities and pupils' sense of disaffection?*

Countering poor **teacher/pupil inter-relations** may involve considering:

- staff training in conflict management

- discussion on consistency of sanctions

- appropriate teacher behaviour and qualities for working with disaffected pupils

Issues

- *What strategies can prevent or reverse pupil perceptions of teacher injustice and lack of respect to pupils?*

- *What are the opportunities for utilising the special skills of teachers who work particularly effectively with disaffected pupils?*

Countering adverse **family factors** may involve considering:

- home-school liaison systems

- communication between staff on troubled pupils

- the management of children in stress

- the merit of a sustained pastoral support role, e.g. counsellor

- multi-agency approaches

Issues

- *How far do schools' current pastoral provision offer sufficient support and time to youngsters with home-related problems?*

- *What is the value of intervention at primary-school level in order to break through parental authentication of inappropriate behaviour or attendance patterns?*

Countering problematic **curriculum and classroom factors** may involve considering:

- the variety of learning tasks made available to pupils

- the issue of differentiation and meeting individual learning needs

- promoting positive learning attitudes

- the consequences of falling behind with work through disaffected behaviour (non-attendance/inattention)

Issues

- *How might teaching styles affect pupil disaffection?*

- *How far is curriculum, and particularly differentiation/ individual learning needs, a key component of strategies for improving behaviour and attendance?*

GLOSSARY of terms (truancy)

BUNKING OFF

KNOCKING OFF

SKIVING

JIGGING

MOGGING

DOGGING

SAGGING

WAGGING

PLAYING THE WAG